CCSS **Genre** Realistic Fiction

W9-AKX-391

? Essential Question
What can learning about different cultures teach us?

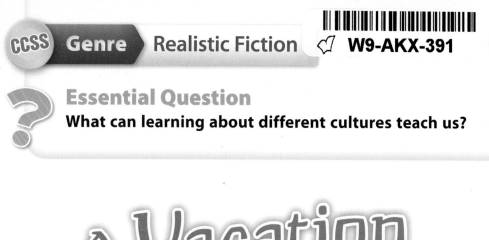

A Vacation in Minnesota

by Hugh Brown
illustrated by Brad Clark

CHAPTER 1
The Land of Lakes

As the airplane began its approach to the airport, Peter looked out of the window. He could see deep-blue lakes and lush green fields below, and it made him feel very excited. This was his first visit to see his cousins in Minnesota, and in fact, apart from a couple of online conversations, he had never met them.

Aiden had promised that, while Peter was there, they would have a picnic floating down a river on inner tubes. Aiden's younger brother, Lars, had said that the county fair would be happening while Peter was there, and he was sure that his prizewinning rabbit was going to win a ribbon again this year. Their older sister, Lynn, had told him they would all go swimming in the lake.

While it all sounded fun, Peter still expected that his vacation in the country would be pretty quiet. He lived in New York City, so even though he did not have any brothers or sisters to play with at home, there was always a lot going on.

Uncle Gunnar was there to meet Peter at the airport. He explained that the airport was on his way home from work and that Peter would meet the rest of the family when they got to the farm. The moment they arrived, Peter's cousins burst out the front door and charged up to the car. Peter suddenly felt shy and unsure of what to say.

"Hey, Peter, how was your flight?" Lars asked.

"What did they give you to eat?" Aiden probed.

Lynn opened the car door for him. "Hi, Peter! Did they show a good movie?" she asked.

Aunt Annika shooed them away. "Quiet, you three—give your cousin a chance to catch his breath! You're worse than the turkeys," she said cheerfully and ushered Peter inside. "I expect you're hungry, Peter."

"Mom expects everyone to be hungry," Lars said, with a smile.

Aunt Annika explained that she had some "hot dish" in the oven and that there was plenty left. "So let me fix you something to eat," she urged. Then she directed Lynn and Aiden to take Peter's bag up to the boys' room. "And Lars— you can do your chores now."

She turned to Peter. "He didn't want to miss you arriving," she explained.

Aunt Annika made Peter sit down at the kitchen table and began to bustle around the kitchen. Soon Peter had a plate piled high with a ground beef casserole topped with crispy potato. He thanked his aunt and tried a small forkful.

"This is really good, Aunt Annika," he exclaimed in appreciation. "This is exactly like Dad makes it."

She chuckled. "Well, you can't come from around these parts without knowing how to make hot dish."

"I thought Dad made it up."

"Oh, no." She explained that hot dish was part of the Minnesotan cultural heritage. When she noticed that Peter's plate was empty, Aunt Annika reached for the serving spoon to give him some more.

"Thanks, but I'm really full, Aunt Annika," Peter said. Then Lynn, Aiden, and Lars came running into the kitchen.

They chimed in unison, "Mom, can we—"

"Yes," their mother interrupted, "off you go, but no swimming without an adult, remember?"

"Come on, Peter," Lynn said. "We'll show you the lake."

CHAPTER 2

Minnesota's "State Bird"

When they got outside, Lars said to Peter, "If you see a flock of strange black birds that kind of hover like hummingbirds, don't wait around. Run as fast as you can for home."

"What are they?" Peter asked cautiously, unsure whether or not Lars was joking.

"Mosquitoes," he said, "as big as your hand! A swarm of them will suck you dry in—"

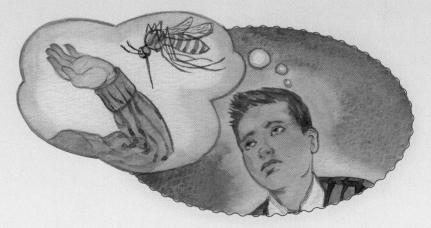

"They will not!" Lynn contradicted with a laugh. She turned to Peter and explained that no one ever listened to a word her younger brother said. She looked thoughtful for a moment and added, "Unless it's about rabbits—they're about the only thing he takes seriously."

"The mosquitoes are pretty bad, though," Aiden said. "It's because of all the lakes where the mosquitoes breed, I suppose. People joke that mosquitoes are Minnesota's state bird, but that's really the loon. We might see one of them on our picnic if we're lucky."

When they arrived at the lake, Lars immediately picked up a stone and skipped it across the water. "I got ten!" he said, jumping up and down. The others picked up stones as well, and Aiden showed Peter how to hold the stone to make it skip. After a few tries, he got it to jump six times.

"That's good," Aiden said. "It took me ages to be able to do that many."

Peter smiled, saying, "You were probably about three years old though, right?" and his cousins all laughed.

"Mosquito alert," Lynn cried suddenly, slapping her arm.

"Let's go," Aiden said, and they all started to run back toward the house.

"Come on, let's go see the rabbits," Lars said. They trooped into the rabbit shed. All the rabbits were white with black noses, ears, and feet.

"They're cute," Peter said. "They sort of remind me of a group of clowns."

"That's because they're Californians—not actually from California—that's just what the breed is called. This is Chester," Lars said proudly, holding up a rabbit and inviting Peter to stroke its thick, silky fur. "It's going to be his big day at the fair tomorrow."

"We'll have to get up at six o'clock to get everything ready," Lars reminded the others. "You don't have to, though," he added quickly to Peter.

"I will," Peter grinned, "but you might have to wake me up."

"Don't worry," Lynn said, rolling her eyes. "Those two are like a stampeding herd of elephants in the morning—there's no way you'll sleep through that."

Peter found out that Lynn was right when he woke the next morning to thumping and crashing, followed by a loud "Shhh!" from one of the cousins. Peter sat up sleepily.

"Oh, are you already awake?" Aiden asked innocently.

Peter quickly got dressed, and the four cousins went out to the sheds. First up was feeding the turkeys.

"They're huge!" Peter exclaimed when he saw them. Suddenly the birds erupted into a deafening chorus of "gobble-gobble-gobble-gobble!"

"I see what your mom meant now," Peter said, "about your talk being worse than the turkeys ..." Unsure of what to say next without offending his cousins, Peter could only stammer, "I mean, uh, that's not, uh, what I mean is ..." but his cousins just laughed. Then all three started saying "gobble-gobble-gobble-gobble," which set the turkeys off again, and soon even Peter was joining in and laughing.

Next they went to the rabbit shed, where Lars explained that they gave each rabbit a small cupful of feed pellets each morning. Peter helped to check that all the animals had hay and fresh water while Lars took Chester out of his cage, brushed him carefully to get rid of any loose fur, and then put him in his traveling box. He explained that they would let Chester get used to the box for a bit before taking him out to the car.

Just then Aunt Annika called them inside for breakfast. She opened the oven and brought out two plates piled high with steaming hot pancakes. She put them in the middle of the table and invited the children to help themselves.

As they were piling up their plates, Uncle Gunnar walked in. "Morning, Peter," he said. "How did you sleep on your first night with the terrible twosome?"

Peter quickly swallowed a mouthful of pancake before answering, "Fine. I slept like a log, and the twosome," he grinned at his cousins, "were as quiet as mice."

"I see you've already been out and about," Uncle Gunnar said.

"Yes, I've been shown all around," Peter confirmed. "It's been really fun."

"Good," Uncle Gunnar smiled. "Do you need a hand with anything, Annika?"

"I'm fine, thanks," Aunt Annika said. "Let's all have some more pancakes." She put fresh pancakes onto Peter's and his cousins' plates to a chorus of thanks, then sat down and took one herself.

CHAPTER 3

The Fair

When they arrived at the fair, they all went with Lars to the pavilion to get Chester settled in before racing back outside to explore the rest of the fair.

"Wait!" Aunt Annika shook her head and laughed as she held the backs of Lars's and Aiden's shirts to make sure they listened to her.

"Monster trucks!" Lars blurted out.

"Kamikaze!" Aiden cried, his head swiveling from side to side as he tried to take in everything around them. Peter laughed with his aunt.

"We'll meet back here at one o'clock for some proper food," she said. "Don't eat too much of all that," she added, letting go of Aiden long enough to wave at the stalls. As they raced off, Aunt Annika called after them, "And stay together—Lynn's in charge!" She gave Lynn a quick hug and told her, "Good luck, dear."

Peter's next few hours went by in a blur. They watched huge four-wheel-drive trucks climb over piles of cars, played carnival games, won prizes, crashed into each other in bumper cars, and went on rides that spun, twisted, and dropped.

After a huge picnic lunch, the family went to the pavilion for the rabbit-judging competition. Everyone waited nervously, but when the winner was announced, it was Chester! The family congratulated Lars as he whooped with joy, and Peter beamed at his cousin, complimenting him on his win.

"Well, I'm not sure how good the competition was this year—the rabbit that came in second wasn't very good," Lars observed.

"Don't be critical, Lars—just enjoy your victory," his mother reminded him gently.

As soon as they got home that evening, Uncle Gunnar took Peter and the cousins to the lake for a quick swim, then they rushed back to feed the animals before supper. After that they washed their hands and sat down at the table to plates piled with turkey and macaroni hot dish with sauerkraut. Peter's aunt explained that she had given him only a small amount of sauerkraut because she was not sure if he liked it.

"Dad eats it all the time, so I'm used to it," Peter said. "It's one of those Scandinavian foods, isn't it? Like *lutefisk* and *lefse*."

"Well, sauerkraut is originally from Germany, but we've always eaten it," Aunt Annika said.

After dinner they went into the living room, where Uncle Gunnar put on some music and Peter's cousins got out board games. It didn't take long, though, before Peter had to admit he was too tired to play, and he went over and sat down on the couch.

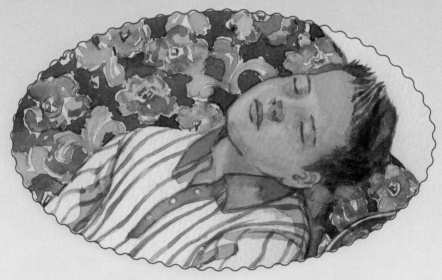

The next thing he knew, Uncle Gunnar was gently waking him from his slumber. "Did I fall asleep?" he asked.

"That's all right. Busy day keeping up with those three," his uncle said.

When Peter woke up again, this time in his bed, it was to the sound of his cousins trying to be quiet as they got dressed to go and feed the animals. "Sorry!" Aiden whispered when Peter sat up.

"It's okay—I want to come, too," Peter replied.

When they finished feeding the animals, they saw Uncle Gunnar getting inner tubes out of the basement. Peter remembered what Aiden had said about the picnic on the river.

CHAPTER 4

Picnic on the River

After another big breakfast, they all got into the car, which had a trailer on the back full of inflated inner tubes. They drove for a few minutes and then stopped at a rest area. Peter wondered if there had been a misunderstanding—were they going to have a picnic and then go to the river?

But when his Uncle Gunnar started taking the tubes off the trailer and Aunt Annika took out a couple of coolers full of food and drinks, Peter asked if they were "there" already. Everyone laughed, and Uncle Gunnar said, "You don't need to go far to find a river around here."

Uncle Gunnar tied the tubes together in a circle, and when he had finished, they all helped carry the "raft" of tubes to the far side of the rest area where the river was. The cousins put the tubes down at the water's edge and put on sunscreen while the adults tied the coolers inside a couple of the tubes.

"We'll all wear life jackets, even though I hear you're a very good swimmer," his aunt said, passing a jacket to Peter and then giving the rest to the other children.

Everyone helped push the raft out into the river and scrambled on as it began to drift away from the shore. The river was slow and shallow, and they floated gently downstream. It was sunny and peaceful—even Peter's cousins had nothing to say for once.

Trying to sound casual, Peter asked if there were ever any alligators spotted around here, and his aunt assured him there were not.

"Wait, there's one," Lars shouted, then with a shriek he slipped off the raft as if he had been pulled under the water, and a moment later, something grabbed hold of Peter's right ankle.

"Help! It's got me!" Peter said, laughing, and he let himself be pulled off the raft, too. Soon all the cousins and Uncle Gunnar were taking turns swimming around and pulling each other into the water.

When it was time for lunch, Aunt Annika began to unpack the coolers. Inside one, there was cold turkey, wild rice salad, berries, and some special dried fish Peter knew was called lutefisk, while the other had juices and a stack of thin flatbread.

"Are they lefse?" Peter asked his aunt.

"Very good," she said approvingly. "Yes, they are. You can use them as wraps for your turkey and salad or put berries in them for dessert—it's up to you."

"Or fill them with lutefisk, turkey, *and* berries," Uncle Gunnar said, grinning as he did just that.

"Dad! That's gross!" his children exclaimed. Their father smiled and took a big bite.

It was silent again while everyone ate, and Peter thought about Sundays at home. He and his dad usually went to their local diner for brunch, and when they got home, he often played on his computer while his dad read the paper. Sundays were usually pretty relaxed. Peter smiled ruefully as he remembered that on the airplane, he had thought that his vacation in the country would be quiet.

When they had finished eating, Lars asked if they could swim over to a nearby island. As soon as Aunt Annika had said yes, Lars jumped up and shouted, "Come on, Peter, let's go!"

Peter grinned, knowing he would miss his cousins when he went back to New York City. But now that he had been to visit them once, he really hoped they would invite him back again soon.

Respond to Reading

Summarize

Use important details from *A Vacation in Minnesota* to summarize what Peter learns about the culture in rural Minnesota. Your graphic organizer may help you.

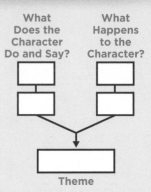

Text Evidence

1. What features of *A Vacation in Minnesota* help you identify it as an example of realistic fiction? GENRE

2. What does Peter learn about himself when he visits his cousins? How does this convey the author's main message? THEME

3. What is the meaning of *stammer* on page 7? Use the cause-and-effect relationship in the paragraph to help you figure out the meaning. CONTEXT CLUES: CAUSE AND EFFECT

4. The author has Peter compare his life in New York City with life in Minnesota on page 15. Write about how this comparison helps express the theme. WRITE ABOUT READING

Compare Texts
Read about Scandinavians in Minnesota.

The Scandinavian State?

The state of Minnesota was originally settled by the Lakota people, and the name Minnesota comes from a Lakota word meaning "sky-colored water."

Many of the first European settlers who came to Minnesota were Scandinavians. People who are called Scandinavian are from the countries of Sweden, Norway, Finland, Iceland, and Denmark, which are in the northern part of Europe.

Water Sports

Minnesota is well known as a great place for water sports. In fact, waterskiing was invented in the state. It's no wonder so many people take to the water there—after all, Minnesota has more than 10,000 lakes!

Traditional Food

Some of the foods that are commonly eaten in Minnesota these days were originally from the homelands of the Scandinavian settlers. Lefse and lutefisk are two examples of these types of foods.

Lefse is a type of Norwegian flatbread that is often made from mashed potato. It is usually eaten as a dessert with butter and sugar.

Lefse (right) and lutefisk (below) are traditional Scandinavian foods.

Lutefisk is another Minnesotan specialty originally from Norway. It is fish that has been dried, soaked in a chemical called lye, and cooked until it is gelatinous. It is often eaten with butter. Many Scandinavian Americans eat this dish at Thanksgiving and Christmas.

The Vikings

The Vikings were originally from Scandinavia. They were great sailors and settled in many countries around Europe during the period from about 800 to 1000 C.E. In fact, some people think that around 1000 C.E., a Viking called Leif Eriksson was the first European to arrive in North America.

The Scandinavians who settled in Minnesota, however, were not Vikings. They settled in America in the late nineteenth century, bringing many aspects of their culture with them.

Syttende Mai

Because of their Scandinavian heritage, Minnesotans celebrate Syttende Mai, which means "the seventeenth of May." On that day in 1814, Norway became an independent country and was no longer ruled by Sweden.

The celebration often includes a parade, dancing, food, art, and music. One town even elects a local man as King of the Trolls during its Syttende Mai festivities.

Make Connections

Why is Minnesota known as the Scandinavian State?
ESSENTIAL QUESTION

Peter's cousins in Minnesota lead a life that is very different from his life in New York City, but some of the food is the same. What do both selections tell you about Scandinavian food? TEXT TO TEXT

Focus on Literary Elements

Dialogue Authors use dialogue to show readers what characters say. Dialogue can help move the plot along and indicate action. Comic strips are an example of the way a story can be told just by using dialogue and illustrations.

Read and Find In this piece of dialogue from page 6, the author tells us what the characters say and what they are doing. As you read it, think about the images that could help tell the story.

"Mosquito alert," Lynn cried suddenly, slapping her arm.

"Let's go," Aiden said, and they all started to run back toward the house.

"Come on, let's go see the rabbits," Lars said. They trooped into the rabbit shed. All the rabbits were white with black noses, ears, and feet.

"They're cute," Peter said. "They sort of remind me of a group of clowns."

Your Turn

Now turn this or another section of dialogue into a comic strip. Use drawings and the words the characters say. Then choose a section without dialogue. Show the action through drawings and create your own dialogue for the characters. Share your comic strip with your classmates.